IMAGES
of America

AROUND THE TOWN OF
SARATOGA

This map shows the town of Saratoga as it appeared on a 1866 map published by S.N. & D.G. Beers and Associates in the *New Topographical Atlas of Saratoga County, New York*. Located in the eastern portion of Saratoga County, the town is bounded on the east by the Hudson River, on the west by Saratoga Lake and the city of Saratoga Springs, on the north by the towns of Wilton and Northumberland, and on the south by the town of Stillwater. Fish Creek flows across the northern portion of town, connecting Saratoga Lake and the Hudson River. The town was originally much larger than it is today; however, its boundaries have remained unchanged since 1819. Saratoga covers some 44,000 acres of land and contains more than 100 miles of town roads. The villages of Schuylerville and Victory are located within the town.

IMAGES
of America

AROUND THE TOWN OF
SARATOGA

Thomas N. Wood III

ARCADIA
PUBLISHING

Published by Arcadia Publishing
Charleston, South Carolina

Library of Congress Catalog Card Number: 2006923702

For all general information contact Arcadia Publishing at:
Telephone 843-853-2070
Fax 843-853-0044
E-mail sales@arcadiapublishing.com
For customer service and orders:
Toll-Free 1-888-313-2665

Visit us on the Internet at www.arcadiapublishing.com

CONTENTS

ACKNOWLEDGMENTS

The photographs in this book cover the period c. 1850 to the present. Most of them are from the collection of the town historian. Many of them were donated by generous friends and residents of the town. One of the most difficult tasks in preparing the book was the selecting of photographs. With so much history and so many photographs, choosing and organizing the material presented a significant challenge. The author would like to thank his mother, Eleanor Wood, the members of the Old Saratoga Historical Association, and the Schuylerville Senior Citizens for their assistance in gathering information used in the book.

INTRODUCTION

Archaeological evidence reveals that the Mohawk branch of the Iroquois inhabited the Saratoga area more than 1,200 years ago. Here, the Native Americans enjoyed excellent fishing and hunting grounds, easily accessed by a network of natural waterways. They were able to travel north and south on the Hudson River, east on the Battenkill River, and west on Fish Creek.

The name Saratoga comes from a Mohawk word: either *Se-rach-ta-gue*, meaning "the hillside country of the quiet river" or "place of the swift water," referring to the rapids and falls that break the stillness of the stream; or *Sa-ra-ta-ke*, meaning "a place where the track of the heel may be seen," referring to nearby rocks that contain footprint-shaped depressions. Either way, Dutch settlers gave the name to the gently rolling land within a region of indefinite boundaries. The region extended roughly from present-day Waterford to the state dam in Northumberland and included land that stretched 6 miles along both sides of the Hudson River.

As early as 1684, a group that included Peter Schuyler obtained the Saratoga Patent, the first title to the land. Bartel Vroman became the first pioneer settler in 1688. Officials at a convention held in Albany on September 4, 1689, resolved that a fort be "made about the house of Bartel Vroman at Sarachtoge." In the summer of 1690, Schuyler, who was then mayor of Albany, cleared a spot in the forest, built a blockhouse for his military stores, and named the place Saratoga. In 1702, Johannes Schuyler settled on lands along Fish Creek, near the present village of Schuylerville. He established farms and erected mills and other buildings as early as 1709. As a way of drawing new people to the area, Schuyler built a garrison house for protection from raids of the French and Indian Wars. Together, Schuyler and the farmers and others who leased or bought land from him formed the town's first major settlement, Fort Saratoga.

In spite of frequent raids, the settlement grew. By the mid-1700s, it included some 30 dwellings with granaries, pens, flour mills, stores, and blacksmith shops, as well as the garrison. On November 17, 1745, a fierce attack destroyed Fort Saratoga. Capt. Peter Schuyler was killed in his own house. Many others were also massacred or taken prisoner. The settlement, including the garrison house, was burned. Fort Saratoga was rebuilt, but attacks continued sporadically during the years of the French and Indian Wars. In 1763, France and England made peace, trouble subsided, and the settlement revived. In 1767, Philip Schuyler erected a flax mill, the first in the American Colonies. In 1770, the Saratoga Reformed Church was organized.

As the country struggled for independence from the British, Saratoga became a focal point of warring activities. Both colonists and loyalists maintained forts, camps, and headquarters within the town. Philip Schuyler, the general in command, used his forces to delay the advance of the British, led by Gen. John Burgoyne. Hostilities intensified in the summer of 1777. On September 10, 1777, Burgoyne's army crossed the Hudson River, halted for a short time, and then headed south. There, the army, one of the mightiest in the world, was defeated in the two battles at Saratoga on September 19 and October 7. Burgoyne retreated back to the village, where he surrendered to Gen. Horatio Gates on October 17. This surrender of British soldiers marked the turning point of the American Revolutionary War. It provided the impetus that caused France to join the American cause against the British.

Saratoga suffered throughout the war. Many of the settlers who chose to stay in the village lost their lives. Others lost their property. Gradually, in the years following the war, the town began to grow and prosper. Flour mills, linen mills, paper mills, and sawmills were constructed. Schools, churches, and businesses were established. The two highways that passed through town, the old Montreal and Albany Military Road and the Saratoga Springs-to-Boston Road, were improved.

The completion of the Champlain Canal in 1822 provided the largest impetus to growth. A boat basin and dry dock were developed, and the town became a major shipping terminal on the canal. Boatloads of potatoes, grain, lumber, hay, and paper originated here. A mule barn was built to house more than 100 mules. As the demand increased, numerous warehouses, hotels, blacksmith shops, and businesses were established. Eventually railroads came, too. By 1882, the Fitchburg Railroad was running through town, connecting Saratoga to Saratoga Springs and Mechanicville and Troy. The Hudson Valley Railway followed in 1899, parallel to the Hudson River. Both railways were abandoned in the 1900s.

Over the years, Saratoga underwent many boundary adjustments. In 1772, the State divided what is now Saratoga County into two districts: Halfmoon and Saraghtoga, which included the present-day town of Easton. Three years later, the State took part of Saraghtoga and made it into a third district, called Ballstown. The New York State Legislature passed an act in 1788 creating towns in place of districts, and from Saratoga took a portion, including Malta, that became the town of Stillwater. The town of Saratoga was still much larger then than it is today. It included all of what in years to come were separated as the towns of Northumberland, Moreau, Wilton, Saratoga Springs, plus parts of the current towns of Greenfield and Corinth. Since 1819, the boundaries of the town of Saratoga have remained the same.

During the first half of the 19th century, two villages were incorporated within the town of Saratoga: Schuylerville, named after the Schuyler family, who were responsible for developing the area in 1831; and Victory, named—as its mills were—in recognition of the American victory during the Battles of Saratoga in 1848. Hamlets, with the names of Coveville, Quaker Springs, Grangerville, and Deans Corners, also developed in Saratoga. In the chapters that follow, these names appear, together with photographs and words that offer understanding and insight into what life was like in Saratoga's historical past. With all the changes, Saratoga has managed to retain its rural character and constant spirit.

One

THE HISTORIC PAST

This famous painting by John Trumbull portrays the turning point of the American Revolutionary War. It shows the surrender at Saratoga of British Gen. John Burgoyne to American commander Gen. Horatio Gates on October 17, 1777. The four figures in the central foreground are, from left to right, Generals Phillips, Burgoyne, and Gates, and Colonel Morgan. At the far right is General Schuyler, who is out of uniform.

Gen. Philip Schuyler commanded the American forces who delayed the advance of General Burgoyne on his march from Montreal toward Albany. Although relieved of his command just prior to the Battles of Saratoga, Schuyler greatly helped the American cause and prepared the way for the defeat of Burgoyne. In more peaceful times, Schuyler was active in both state and national government and was a prominent local businessman. He and his family were instrumental in the development of the Schuylerville area.

Catherine Van Rensselaer Schuyler was the wife of Gen. Philip Schuyler. She assisted her husband in his efforts to delay the British and keep them from obtaining needed supplies. She is best known for setting fire to her wheat fields so that General Burgoyne could not gather the grain he needed.

Johannes Schuyler, grandfather of Gen. Philip Schuyler, acquired his vast Saratoga property in 1702. He induced several families from Albany to settle in the Saratoga area. He improved his property by erecting mills and farms. On November 28, 1745, his house, fort, and holdings were burned during a raid of the French and Indian War. Another Philip Schuyler, an uncle of the general, was killed in the raid. Some 12 years later, the Philip who became general settled on the property.

Fort Saratoga was located on the west side of the Hudson River, on the flats south of the village of Schuylerville. Burned and rebuilt three times, the structure was known as Fort Vrooman in 1689, Fort Saratoga in 1702 and in 1721 when rebuilt by Philip Livingston, and Fort Clinton in 1746 when rebuilt and named for the state's governor.

Fort Hardy was the site where General Burgoyne's troops surrendered, or "grounded," their arms in 1777. Named after the royal governor of the province, Fort Hardy was built in 1757. The bricks used in its construction came from Fort Edward and were brought down the Hudson River in bateaux. Fort Hardy covered some 15 acres of land on the flats north of Fish Creek. The largest and most elaborate of any of the forts around Schuylerville, Fort Hardy was used as a shelter for troops and as a depot for supplies.

Alexander Hamilton visited Saratoga frequently. A prominent statesman, he served as secretary of the treasury. In December 1780, he married Gen. Philip Schuyler's daughter, Elizabeth. Hamilton was killed in a duel with Vice President Aaron Burr in 1804.

Elizabeth Schuyler met Alexander Hamilton at the Morristown, New Jersey, encampment during the winter of 1779–80. After a short courtship, she accepted his offer of marriage. She was the only one of General Schuyler's daughter who married with her father's consent. The wedding took place in December 1780, in the drawing room of the Schuyler house in Albany that the Hamiltons visited on numerous occasions.

The original Gen. Philip Schuyler House was destroyed by fire in 1777. Gen. John Burgoyne ordered his men to burn the house, following a night of partying on their retreat from defeat at the Battles of Saratoga. The house was rebuilt in November of the same year. Today, it is owned and maintained by the National Park Service. Located in the village of Schuylerville, the house is furnished and open to the public during the summer months.

Schuyler's sawmill was located on the banks of Fish Creek in Smithville. Spared by the retreating British, the mill was used to saw the lumber for rebuilding the Schuyler House in November 1777.

14

For more than 100 years, the Stover family owned and occupied the Schulyer House. George Stover, son of longtime Saratoga resident John Stover, purchased the Schuyler House in 1838. More than three generations of Stovers lived in the house. In 1952, when the family moved out, many of the household goods were sold at the public auction shown in this photograph.

Originally, the Schuyler House did not include the large front porch shown here. Added later, the porch stayed for many years until the National Park Service removed it.

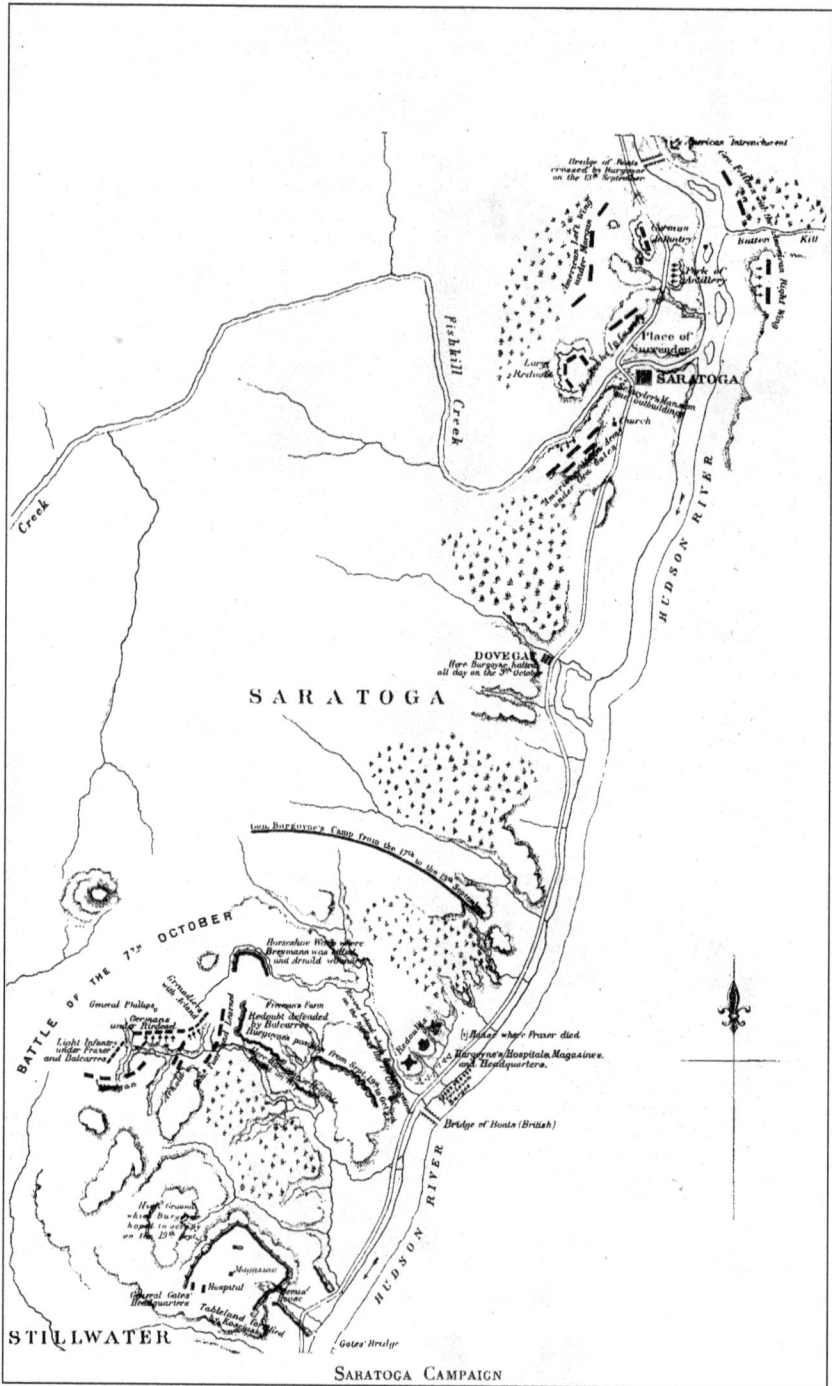

SARATOGA CAMPAIGN

This map shows the location of the battlefield and the surrender area at Saratoga. After being defeated in the Battles of Saratoga, the British retreated north, with the idea of going back to Canada. They were outmaneuvered, however, by the American forces who surrounded them and prevented them from either heading north or crossing the Hudson River.

16

Gen. Horatio Gates commanded the American forces at the Battles of Saratoga, and it was to him that General Burgoyne surrendered his sword. Gates was appointed by George Washington to replace Gen. Philip Schuyler in the days immediately preceding the Battles at Saratoga. When Gates arrived in camp to take command of the American forces, Schuyler offered him information and help. Gates chose to ignore both. However, Gates reaped the benefits of Schuyler's earlier tactic of slowing General Burgoyne's advance toward Albany.

Gen. Philip Schuyler planned the defensive campaign that resulted in Burgoyne's defeat at Saratoga. He led the American forces that impeded General Burgoyne's advance toward Albany. Born in 1733, Schuyler was a personal friend of George Washington and served under him as major general of the Northern Department from 1775–77. During his illustrious career, Schuyler also served as a member of the Continental Congress, senator from New York State, chairman of the Board of Indian Commissioners, surveyor general of New York State, and president of two canal companies. A victim of constant ill health, he died in 1804. The village of Schuylerville was named after him and his family.

Gen. Benedict Arnold was an active leader in the Battles of Saratoga. Later, he became one of the most famous traitors of all times by defecting to the British side. He deserted the Americans because they denied him the recognition and promotions he desired.

Col. Daniel Morgan was the commander of the American sharpshooters who inflicted serious damage to the advancing British army. His men killed Gen. Simon Fraser, a leader of the British military effort.

Gen. John Burgoyne was commander of the British army that left Montreal in 1777 with a goal of uniting in Albany with Gen. William Howe. Howe was to come up the Hudson River from New York City. The British plan was to conquer New York State and divide the colonies. Burgoyne's southward advance was stopped at the Battles of Saratoga. He and his 5,700 troops surrendered at Saratoga on October 17, 1777.

Gen. Baron Friedrich von Riedesel was the commander of more than 3,000 German troops that were a part of Burgoyne's army. This regiment fought at Ticonderoga, Hubbardtown, Freeman's Farm, and Bemis Heights.

Crown forces under the command of Lt. General John Burgoyne

American forces under the command of Major General Horatio Gates

Fortifications

Site of Sword Ceremony – Lt. General Burgoyne surrenders to Major General Horatio Gates.

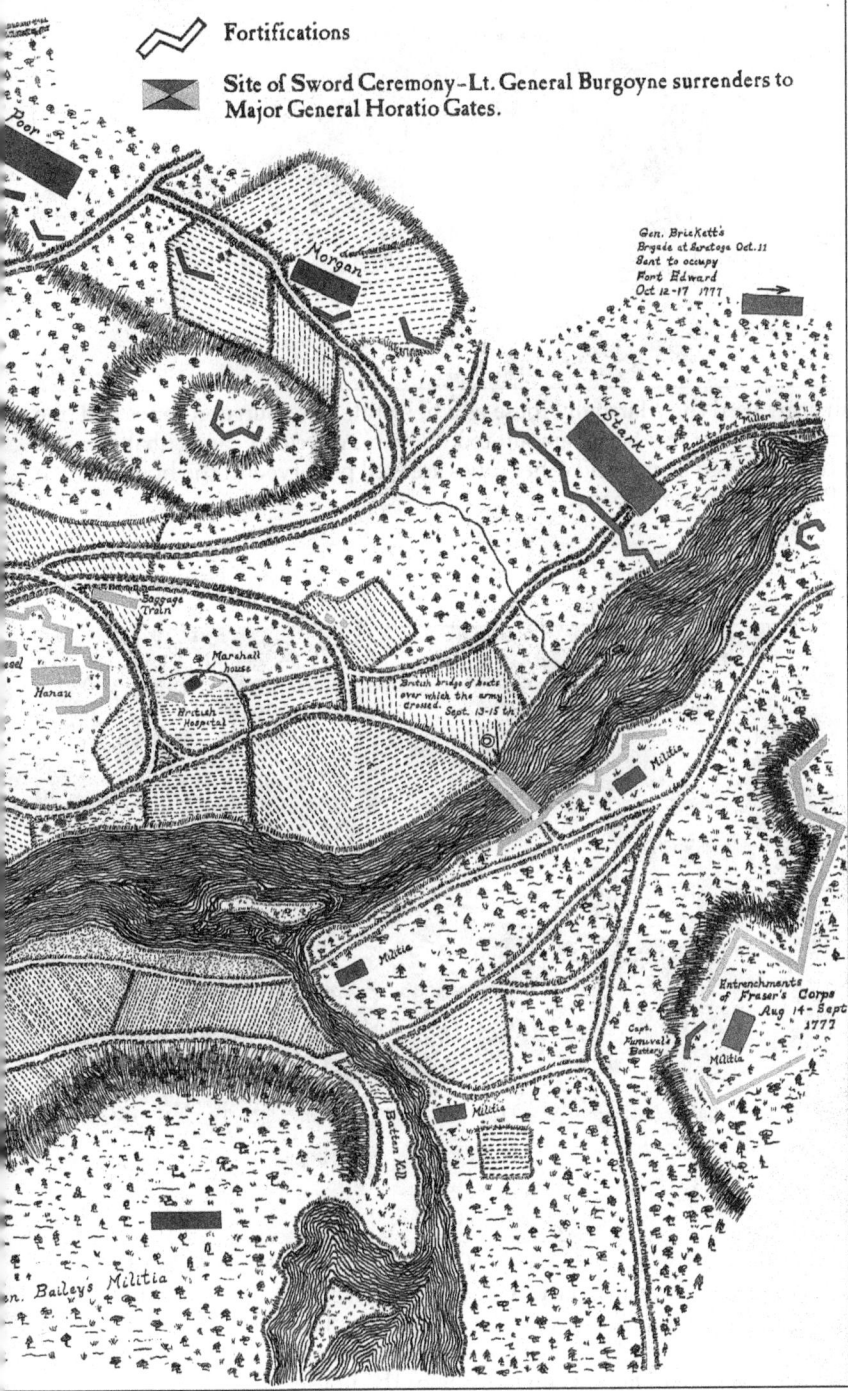

Gen. Brickett's
Brigade at Saratoga Oct. 11
Sent to occupy
Fort Edward
Oct 12-17 1777

Morgan

Stark

Road to Fort Miller

Baggage
Train

Marshall
house

British
Hospital

Hanau

Bridge of boats
over which the army
crossed Sept. 13-15 th

Militia

Militia

Militia

Entrenchments
of Fraser's Corps
Aug 14 - Sept
1777

Capt.
Pausch's
Battery

Militia

Militia

Boston Rd.

Militia

Bailey's Militia

This map shows the British and American position s at Saratoga from October 10–17, 1777. The Americans totally surrounded the British: General Stark blocked a retreat to the north by positioning cannons on the high ground, later called Stark's Knob; General Morgan prevented a retreat to the west; General Poor stood in the way of a retreat to the east; and General Gates blocked the advance to the south.

21

The retreating British army used the Marshall House as a hospital. Here Surgeon Jones had one leg shot away while the other leg was being amputated. Eleven American cannonballs passed through the house. The splintered beams and other relics are well preserved in the house, which was built in 1773 by Peter Lansing of Albany.

The Marshall House, located on Route 4 just north of the village of Schuylerville, still looks much as it did at the time of the Revolutionary War. Renovations since that time have only slightly altered its appearance. General Burgoyne's army used the basement of he house as a hospital for wounded officers in October 1777. Attacked by American cannon fire, the building sustained numerous shots. The Bullard family currently owns the house.

Madam Riedesel nursed the wounded British officers in the cellar of the Marshall house in October 1777. She was the wife of Major General Reidesel, who commanded the German troops under General Burgoyne.

During the week of October 10–17, 1777, Madam Reidesel and her children took refuge from the American cannon fire in the lowest area of the Marshall House. Shown here is a bunk in the cellar, where the mother and her three little girls stayed until after Burgoyne's surrender.

En route to the battlefield at Bemis Heights, General Burgoyne used the Dovegat House as his headquarters while his troops encamped around it the night of September 15, 1777. Later, on his retreat, Burgoyne halted and breakfasted here. The Dovegat House was located on the brink of the Champlain Canal, just a short distance north of the hamlet of Coveville, which was originally called Dovegat.

The former parsonage of the Dutch Reformed church stood throughout the Revolutionary War period. Built in the 1770s, the parsonage is the oldest house within the village Schuylerville. Located on Route 4 on the northern edge of the village, the building is now known as the Burton House.

The surrender of British Gen. John Burgoyne to American Gen. Horatio Gates took place on October 17, 1777, along the main road south of Saratoga, on property owned by Gen. Philip Schuyler. This view of the surrender area is from the southwest entrenchment wall of Fort Hardy.

Near this tree, known as Surrender Tree, the Articles of Capitulation were drawn up and signed on October 16, 1777. In the articles, General Burgoyne, commander of the mightiest army of the time, agreed to the terms of surrender. The Saratoga event is recognized as one of the 15 most decisive victories in world history because it marked the turning point of the American Revolutionary War. It provided the impetus for the French to join the American cause against the British. Surrender Tree was located in what is now Sulli's parking lot on the east side of lower Broadway in Schuylerville. Walking canes were made from the tree when it died.

Fort Hardy was the field of grounded arms. At this site, some 8,000 British and German troops piled their rifles and surrendered their cannons to the Americans.

Here, on October 17, 1777, Gen. John Burgoyne surrendered his sword to Gen. Horatio Gates. All of Burgoyne's troops marched past this location, just south of Saratoga, on their way to Massachusetts.

The plaque marking the surrender of General Burgoyne is shown on the hill at the right of Route 4, south of the village of Schuylerville. Visible at the left are the Hudson Valley trolley tracks, which once ran from Troy to Glens Falls.

This painting shows Burgoyne's troops marching in defeat past the victorious Americans. The tune *Yankee Doodle* was played as the British went by. The defeat at Saratoga was especially humiliating because the mightiest army in the world had to surrender to a group of rebels who were fighting for their freedom.

The Saratoga Monument commemorates the surrender of Burgoyne's army at the close of one of the 15 most decisive battles in the world. It stands on the site of Burgoyne's fortified camp on the hill, overlooking the place of his surrender. Completed in June 1883, it stands 154 feet high on a 40-foot-square base, with 190 steps leading to the top.

The cornerstone of the Saratoga Monument was laid with civic and military ceremonies on October 17, 1877, the 100th anniversary of the surrender of General Burgoyne to General Gates.

28

The actual monument was built a few feet away from the site shown here at the cornerstone dedication. Located in the village of Victory, it was erected by the Saratoga Monument Association and is owned and managed by the National Park Service.

Scene at the Dedication of the Saratoga Battle Monument Schuylerville Oct 18th 1912

Dignitaries from throughout the state and the nation were among the large crowd that attended the dedication of the Saratoga Monument in October 1912. The dedication included ceremonies and historical pageants. Local high school students and adults re-enacted the events that occurred during the historic battle and surrender.

New York Gov. John A. Dix spoke at the dedication of the Saratoga Monument on October 18, 1912. Dix owned an estate in the town of Greenwich, located just north of Schuylerville, across the Hudson River.

The 10th U.S. Cavalry put on many demonstrations and participated in ceremonies and pageants during Saratoga's Historical Week in October 1912.

In one of the activities during Historical Week of 1912, the 10th U.S. Cavalry conducted military demonstrations in the field just east of the Saratoga Monument, shown above. The cavalry exhibitions attracted large crowds of spectators.

Camp Scene
10th U.S. Cavalry, Historical Week Schuylerville 191

The 10th U.S. Cavalry camped in the villages of Schuylerville and Victory during Historical Week of October 1912. The camps were open to the public at various times of day. Local residents, young and old, visited the camps to learn about the cavalry's daily procedure and work.

The 10th U.S. Cavalry paraded through the village of Schuylerville during Historical Week of October 1912. Large crowds gathered all along the main street to watch.

Men dressed in Revolutionary War uniforms marched through town during Historical Week of 1912. Visitors came from all over the state and nation to attend the events. Travelers arrived here on the Boston and Maine Railroad and the Hudson Valley Trolley.

Residents wore their best clothes when they went out to view or participate in Historical Week celebrations of 1912. Pictured here, fifth from the left, is Mabel Orr.

33

1022 British Gun — Schuylerville, N.Y.

This British cannon from the War of 1812 was located on the monument grounds. It was donated to the Monument Association by John Watts DePeyster. In the 1970s, it was moved to Ft. Niagara by New York State.

1023 Schuylerville—From top of monument overlooking Burgoyne's Camp

From the windows at the top of the Saratoga Monument, the view covers nearly all of the area in which the historic events surrounding the Battles of Saratoga and General Burgoyne's surrender took place. Shown here is the view eastward, overlooking Burgoyne's campsite.

The Saratoga Monument was illuminated during the nights of Education Week in 1926. The illumination made it possible to see the monument for miles. The effort involved in providing the electricity and lights reflected the celebration's importance and value to the state and local community.

34

Two

THE TOWN OF SARATOGA

Agriculture has always been a vital and important part of Saratoga's economy. Although dairy farming predominates, there are many fruit, vegetable, and horse farms in town. Current agricultural practices reflect the national trend of fewer and larger farms. Now torn down, this typical, large farm barn was once located on Walsh Road.

Area farmers grew and thrashed grain on their farms. They commonly grew wheat, oats, rye, and barley. They used the grain primarily for animal feed. Pictured, from left to right, are Philip Lasher, Andrew King, John Snyder, unidentified, Harry Loupe, and unidentified. At the far left was the source of power: a horse treadmill.

In the early days, hay was handled in the loose form and was placed on the wagon, either by hand or with a hay loader. Here, Thomas N. Wood Sr. stands on top of his wagonload of hay at his farm in the hamlet of Grangerville.

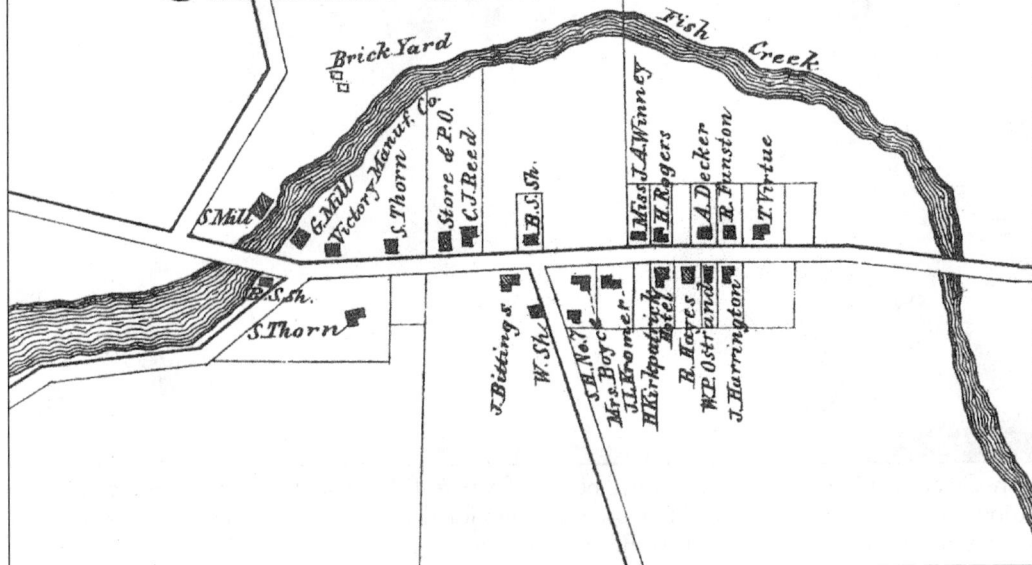

GRANGERVILLE

This 1866 map from the *New Topographical Atlas of Saratoga County, New York*, shows the hamlet of Grangerville. As early as Revolutionary War times, there were mills in the area. The hamlet was named for Harvey Granger, an early resident who ran the local gristmill for many years. In the mid-1800s, the hamlet included more than 30 residences and businesses. Located 2 miles west of Schuylerville, Grangerville has fewer houses today, perhaps 20.

Caswell Ham's store and gristmill were located in the hamlet of Grangerville. The mill received much of its power from a waterwheel, fed by water impounded by a large dam. Each autumn, traps that were set at the dam caught barrels of eels. The eels were sold to merchants in New York City.

Fish Creek in Grangerville has always been a favorite fishing spot. Native Americans once enjoyed excellent fishing here. They used to camp for the summer at a location near the area shown in this picture. On the left is the gristmill, with the dam in the background.

The gristmill in Grangerville was built by Jesse Toll, who sold it to Harvey Granger. Other owners of the mill included a man named Benedict, John K. Proper, Samuel Slocom, John Chapman, George Newland, Otis Thorne, Daniel Deyoe, B.J. Thorne, Elmer Baker, and Caswell Ham.

One of the owners of the Grangerville gristmill was Elmer Baker. Millers who operated the mill for Baker over the years included Michael Mezerra, a Mr. Berry, and Eber Sage. On June 8, 1938, the Grangerville gristmill burned in a fire sparked by the backfire of an engine that was being used as a supplemental source of power.

The Elmer Baker house was located in Grangerville, on the south side of Route 29, at the site of the Thomas Poultry Farm. It was destroyed by fire in 1955. Baker, who owned and operated the Grangerville gristmill, also purchased the Grangerville Hotel, next door to his home. No guests ever came to the hotel, so Baker ended up tearing it down. The story is that people stayed away because bloodstains kept reappearing on the ballroom wall no matter how many times it was repainted. The bloodstains dated from the death of a man named Rodney Granger, who shot and killed himself in the hotel.

The Saratoga Creamery operated on Wall Street in Grangerville at the same plant that currently serves as a woodworking facility. For many years, the creamery processed milk from area farms and made thousands of pounds of butter. The creamery gave local residents free buttermilk, a by-product of the butter-manufacturing process. Later, Fairlawn Farms of New Jersey bought the plant, expanded it, and turned it into a transfer facility. The company collected milk from local farms and trucked it to Fairlawn, New Jersey. In 1963, the milk plant closed.

Pictured here are employees of Victory Mill preparing to serve a meal at a company picnic. The mill owned and operated a guest house for its workers on Hughes Road, just south of Grangerville. Now privately owned, the guest house operates as a bed-and-breakfast establishment.

In June 1950, an airplane crashed on the Thomas Wood farm in Grangerville. The unlicensed pilot, a young man from New Jersey, suffered only a broken leg. Hundreds of curious people came to inspect the wreckage, and the plane was looted before the insurance company's truck arrived to pick it up.

This 1866 map shows the residences and businesses of Quaker Springs. This hamlet, located near the center of Saratoga, was named after the religious group who came to the area for its mineral springs. The Quakers, officially known as the Society of Friends, settled here c. 1765. They held services in a log structure until 1793, when they built frame meetinghouse.

Wrights Sawmill was the source of much of the lumber used in the construction of buildings in Quaker Springs. The sawmill was one of several nonresidential structures in Quaker Springs c. 1900. Others included a post office, an Episcopal church, and a large general store. The store was owned by Arthur and Violet Ellis when it burned on October 2, 1962.

This view is looking west on Main Street in Quaker Springs. A 1871 directory lists the following persons working in Quaker Springs: a harness maker, wagon maker, blacksmith, shoemaker, doctor, lawyer, hotel keeper, preacher, and postmaster/general merchandiser. By 1900, the population numbered 150. The school at the corner of Ruckytuck Road and Route 32 was closed in the late 1940s, after the formation of the Schuylerville Central School District.

The Banner Store, Lohnes Brothers, Quaker Springs, N. Y.

This picture shows the Banner Store of Quaker Springs in 1911, when it was owned and operated by the Lohnes Brothers. The store was previously owned by S.F. Bradt. In 1863, Bradt was succeeded by Isaac W. Meader. The post office was moved from the hotel to the store, and Meader became store owner and postmaster. On November 8, 1908, the post office closed.

This view shows the Quaker Springs Hotel and Mineral Springs. The springs drew many visitors, who drank the water for medicinal purposes. The mineral water from the springs was bottled and sold for a time.

The Methodist Episcopal Church of Quaker Springs was incorporated in 1843, built in 1844, and dedicated in 1845. Its six stained-glass windows (from Utica Stained-Glass Works) were added in 1899. Two other Methodist Churches combined with Methodist Episcopal in 1935 and, today, the congregation remains a central and active part of the community.

The Mineral Spring in Quaker Springs contains lime, magnesium, and iron, with carbonic gas and salts of sodas. The water of the springs is charged with natural gas and is of very high quality. A second spring, located about 25 feet northeast of the main spring, contains a lot of sulfur.

E.R. Meader made his home in Quaker Springs. He was the brother of carpenter Isaac W. Meader, who built the Quaker Springs Hotel, owned and operated the general store, and served as postmaster.

The Dodd homestead was located on Route 32, south of the hamlet of Quaker Springs. For many years, the Dodd family operated two dairy farms. They eventually sold the farms and discontinued farming.

The John Kirkpatrick house was the first home built by local carpenter Isaac W. Meader. It was located in the hamlet of Quaker Springs.

46

Larmon's Bridge was a steel-frame, plank-floor bridge which carried Burgoyne Road across Fish Creek. In the 1960s, this one-lane span was replaced by a new bridge.

STAFFORD'S
BRIDGE, FISH CREEK

Stafford's Bridge carried Route 67 over Fish Creek. A marina with boat rentals was located on each side of bridge. During its construction, the steel-frame truss bridge collapsed at one point but miraculously, no one was injured. Stafford's Bridge was replaced in 1967.

This view of Fish Creek is from Route 68, near Stafford's Bridge. Fishing was excellent in this area. One of the marinas that offered picnicking and boat rentals is barely visible behind the trees.

River Run Farm on Fitch Road dates back to 1798. In that year, Ebenezer Fitch settled on this farm. Subsequent owners have improved the property over the years.

A large sign located in the village of Schuylerville listed the names of "men of the town of Old Saratoga serving in the armed forces." The Honor Roll was erected at the south end of Broad Street. It is no longer there.

This slaughterhouse and rendering plant emitted strong odors at times. The plant, located west of Schuylerville just off Route 29, was destroyed by fire in the early 1950s. The cause of the Sunday morning fire was never determined.

Kenneth Bullard's warehouse was built on the banks of the Champlain Canal, just north of the village of Schuylerville. Located on the east side of Route 4, the building was used for apple packing and cold storage.

This aerial view of Bullard Apple Orchards shows a bunkhouse for farm workers on the left and two other buildings used for storage and maintenance. Bullard Orchards began operating some 100 years ago. Dr. Bullard was one of the first owners. Bullard was followed by his son Kenneth, who in turn was succeeded by his son David. The orchard is currently operated by Nate Darrow.

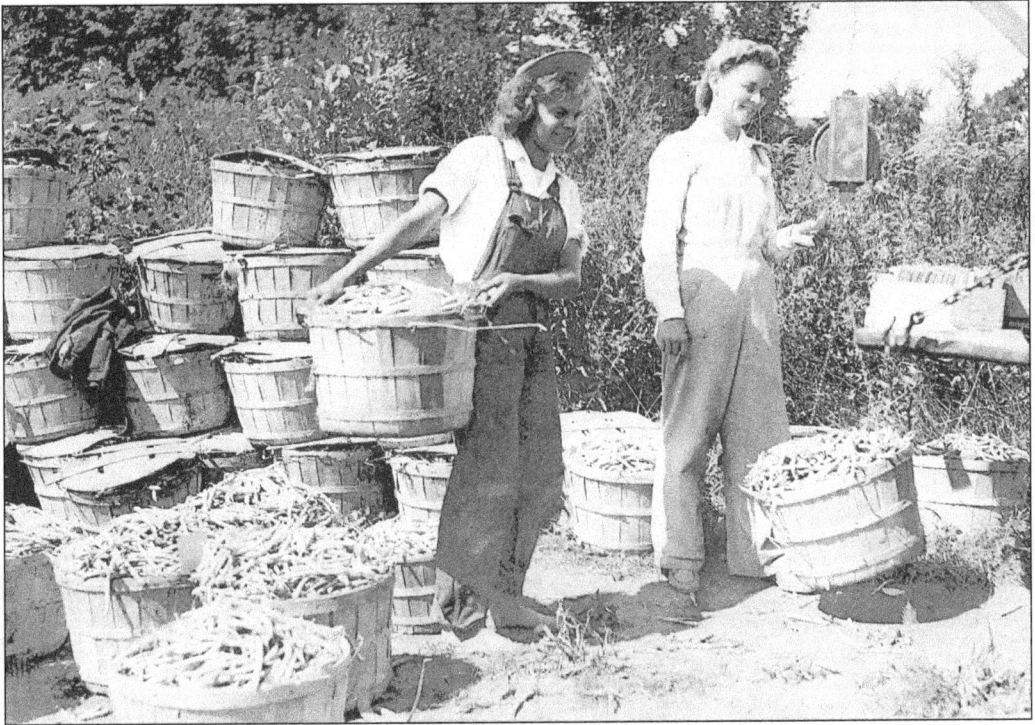

During the World War II years, students of Skidmore College in Saratoga Springs worked summers on the Kenneth Bullard farm picking vegetables. Here they are shown picking and packing string beans on the farm in Saratoga.

The Champlain Canal was important in the economic development of the Saratoga area. This aerial view shows Lock 5 of the canal in Saratoga, just north of the village of Schuylerville.

Aqueducts had to be constructed to carry the Champlain Canal over local streams. The aqueduct shown here takes the canal and the towpath across a stream in Saratoga.

View up the Hudson Valley

This view shows the Champlain Canal running between Schuylerville and Coveville. On the left is the Hudson Valley Trolley line, and on the right is the Hudson River. Completed in 1822, the canal connected Waterford to Whitehall. The waterway was widened several times.

Schuylerville. N.Y. 536

Then, in 1917, the route of the canal was moved to the Hudson River, connecting Waterford to Fort Edward.

This aerial view, c. 1952, shows Garnsey's Airfield and Racetrack, located south of Schuylerville. The photograph was taken looking west-southwest.

The Sarle homestead stands off Route 4, near the hamlet of Coveville. Coveville is located 3 miles south of Schuylerville on a cove in the Hudson River—hence, its name. The area was originally named Dovegat after a prominent early settler.

The original town Highway Department Garage was built in the late 1930s on the south side of Route 32, between the village of Victory and the hamlet of Quaker Springs. In 1997, a new garage was built to replace it on the same Saratoga site.

In 1913, the Hudson River flooded this valley south of the village of Schuylerville. Spring floods were common in Saratoga until the Conklinville Dam was completed and Sacandoga Lake started to be filled in March 1930. After that, the dam created a huge reservoir which held back massive quantities of water, thereby eliminating the traditional floods.

This farm is typical of those once located throughout the town of Saratoga, where farming was an early and long-enduring way of life. Agriculture is still important to Saratoga. Dairy farms, horse farms, vegetable farms, and fruit farms still exist.

Three

THE VILLAGE OF SCHUYLERVILLE

This map of Schuylerville shows the residences and businesses that were part of the village in 1866. The map is from the *New Topographical Atlas of Saratoga County, New York.*

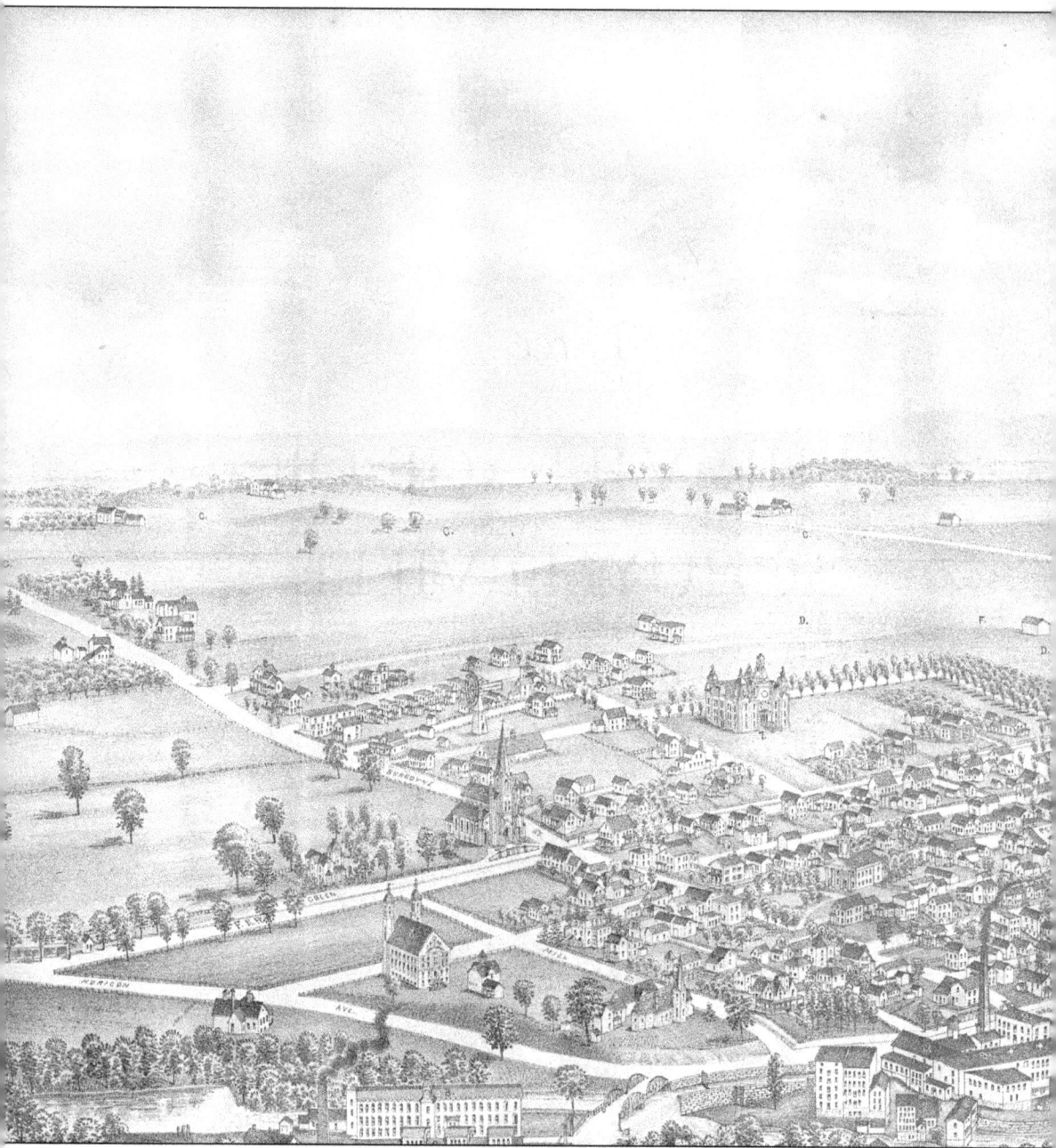

This 1889 lithographic map of the village of Schuylerville shows in detail the structures and features of the village. At that time, both the Champlain Canal and the Fitchburg Railroad ran

through the village.

These two views show South Broad Street in Schuylerville, looking north. The picture at the top was taken before 1900; this is known because the trolley tracks that later ran down the center of the street had not yet been installed. In 1912, Broad Street was paved with bricks. The lower view is from the mid-1920s; note that the trolley tracks are present and the street is paved with bricks.

BUSINESS SECTION, BROAD STREET,
SCHUYLERVILLE, N.Y

Broad Street was the main street in the village of Schuylerville. It was a beehive of activity. Anything that people needed could be purchased on Broad Street. These two views are looking south from the intersection of Ferry Street. The top one is from the mid-1930s, and the lower one is c. 1910.

This pre-1900 picture shows Saratoga Street, looking west from the intersection of Broad Street. On the left is Shepard's store.

Taken from the top of the Saratoga Monument, this eastward view shows the village of Schuylerville below. The 154-foot monument stands on top of a high hill, offering clear-day views of areas as distant as 100 miles.

Snowstorms were common in Schuylerville, and this one in 1914 was especially heavy. The view at the top shows the Hudson Valley Trolley, equipped with a snowplow, clearing the tracks on Broad Street near the Schuylerville House (in front of the present site of the Glens Falls National Bank). The view below, looking north, was taken from the west side of Broad Street, across from the Bullard Building.

Two bridges cross Fish Creek at the southern end of Schuylerville. The Fish Creek Bridge, on the right, and the trolley bridge on the left. This view shows the Hudson Valley Trolley crossing the 270-foot-long, steel-plate girder bridge. From 1900 to 1928, some 35 trolley cars per day passed through the village.

The railroad reached Schuylerville in 1882. Shown here are some of the workers who laid the track. The line that originally served the village was the Fitchburg Railroad. Later, it was replaced by the Boston and Maine, which in turn was replaced by the Saratoga and Schuylerville Railroad. The line was abandoned here in 1955.

The railroad track ran down the middle of Green Street, as is shown in this view, looking south.

Workers laid the trolley tracks on Broad Street in 1900. This photograph was taken near the intersection of Ferry Street, looking north.

This photograph was taken facing south on Broad Street, near Spring Street. It shows the progress made on the trolley tracks in 1900.

This aerial view, c. 1950, shows the Hotel Schuyler in the village of Schuylerville. The hotel was originally called the Goldsmith House. It opened in 1868 with a grand Masonic Ball. Over the years, the hotel hosted many notable people.

This tree-lined street in Schuylerville had a good, wide sidewalk. The picture, c. 1900, was taken looking north on Church Street.

The hurricane of 1950 did extensive damage in Schuylerville. Looking north, this photograph shows numerous uprooted trees blocking Broad Street, near the intersection of Saratoga Street.

The hurricane of 1950 not only uprooted trees but also tore roofs off buildings. This photograph shows Broad Street, near Sulli's Market.

In 1952, Schuylerville celebrated the Fourth of July with this parade. Bullard Orchards employee Elwaine Booth is shown driving the company's new tractor and apple sprayer along Broad Street, near the intersection of Ferry Street.

In 1831, toll bridges were constructed across the Hudson River to take the place of ferry service. Tolls were charged to cross this bridge at Schuylerville. For horse-drawn vehicles the tolls were as follows: one-horse vehicle, 10¢s; two-horse vehicle, 15¢; and for each extra horse, 2¢. The toll for a score of sheep was 20¢, and for a score of cattle 40¢. Foot passengers paid only 2¢. In 1884, total receipts came to $2,847.46. The bridge was built with private capital, under state charter. It consisted of iron trusses, plank flooring, 14 iron-corded bents, and 12 stone piers. The span was 818 feet long, 20 feet wide, and stood 18 feet above the water. The tollhouse, built at a cost of $300, was located on an island between two sections of the bridge. Often damaged by floods, the bridge underwent frequent repairs. In 1901, the toll bridge went into receivership and, in 1910, it became a free bridge.

Pictured here on a winter day are four workmen building a bridge across the Hudson River. This bridge was one of two steel-framed spans built across the Hudson River at Schuylerville in the early 1900s. Both were one-lane bridges with plank flooring. The planks created a considerable rumble when vehicles passed over them.

These photographs show the first of two one-lane bridges leading over the Hudson River at Schuylerville. In the view above, cars are heading east, away from the village. The tollhouse is visible on the left. In the view below, cars are heading west on Route 29, toward Schuylerville. The tollhouse is on the right. The last family to live in the house was the Kelly family.

The old wooden bridges of the 1900s had to be dismantled before the new Hudson River bridges could be built. These photographs show the dismantling under way. The eastern bridge (left) was taken down in 1958.

By the middle of 1958, crews were constructing the two new bridges over the Hudson River at Schuylerville. The bridges were a significant improvement to the area. They were wider, safer, quieter, and much stronger than the earlier bridges, and they could accommodate the heavy truck traffic that used Route 29.

The Hotel Schuyler accommodated up to 500 people. Over the years, its guests included many patrons of the nearby racetrack in Saratoga Springs. The hotel was popular accommodation for visitors to the race track in Saratoga Springs. Originally called the Goldsmith House, the hotel was built in 1868 and stood until 1997, when it was destroyed in a fire.

The municipal bathing beach in Schuylerville was a popular swimming area. Completed in 1934, the beach was part of a Works Progress Administration federal assistance project. This view shows the beach during a time of flooding.

Constructed in the late 1800s, this building at different times housed the local bank and the local newspaper, the *Schuylerville Standard*. It is located on the corner of Ferry and Broad Streets. Plesko's Beauty Parlor and Barber Shop were located in this building. The Winter Club used to meet in the upstairs for dances and parties.

"First-class table and board"—that was how the American House Hotel was advertised when it opened on South Broad Street in the late 1800s. The hotel was a popular rendezvous for village businessmen. In the early 1900s, John J. Hughes owned the hotel and advertised room rates of $2 per night.

This feed store on the corner of Green and Spring Streets had a number of different owners. Owners included William G. Ruff, Art Parks, and the Gronziek family. In the mid-1800s, before it became a store, the building was a lantern factory. In the early 1970s, the building was destroyed by fire. Presently located on the site are the Schuylerville Fire Department and the Village of Schuylerville Offices.

The Bullard Paper Mill was established in 1863 on South Broad Street. In 1870, the mill was heavily damaged by fire. When the paper mill went out of business, the Town of Saratoga

purchased the original office building and used it for municipal offices. The building burned in the mid-1970s. The land was deeded to Schuylerville and developed as a village park.

The Red Lion Inn was located on Broad Street. It later became Quality Hall, a furniture store. Later still, it served as the home of the Schuylerville American Legion. The Grand Union Company bought it from the American Legion, tore it down, and built a grocery store on the site in the 1950s.

This picture of the Champlain Canal dates from 1900. The view, looking south, shows the towpath on the left and the St. Nicholas Hotel in the background.

The original Bullard Paper Mill office was bought by the Town of Saratoga for use as a municipal office after the mill closed. Located on South Broad Street, the office burned in the mid-1970s. Subsequently deeded to Schuylerville, the property now serves as a park.

The Schuyler Hose Company extinguished a fire at the Broadway theater in the mid-1950s. The theater was damaged but not destroyed. The building later became a restaurant and bar, which operated until the mid-1980s, when another fire occurred. The second fire destroyed the building.

This early 1900s photograph of the Schuyler Hose Company shows its members on parade, in full uniform. One of the members carrying a horn is identified as a Mr. Barrett. The Hose Company is the fire department of Schuylerville and is one of three departments within the town of Saratoga. The other two are the David Nevins Fire Department of Victory and the Quaker Springs Fire Company. The General Schuyler Rescue Squad serves the entire town.

In 1941, the Schuylerville Fire Department Fife and Drum Corps assembled for this photograph. The view is looking east on Church Street, across from the old firehouse. A fire truck is visible behind the men.

E. McMahon owned and operated a drugstore in Schuylerville. This photograph taken in 1875 shows the clean, orderly, and well-illuminated interior of the store. The business was located on Broad Street.

The Baptist church was erected at the corner of Church and Ferry Streets in 1833. The 30-by-60-foot building had a seating capacity of 250, with a Sunday school that accommodated an additional 50 people. The church closed in 1926. In the years that followed, the building was used for the storage of apples. This photograph shows the building in the process of being demolished.

Philip Schuyler donated his land on Church Street as a site for the Methodist Episcopal Church of Schuylerville. Established in 1826, the church contains the oldest operating pipe organ in the community.

This interior view of the Methodist Episcopal church shows the historic pipe organ on the right. Built in England more than 200 years ago, the organ was used at Kings Chapel in Boston in the years before the American Revolutionary War. The Reverend J.M. Webster is at the pulpit in this 1883 photograph.

When the Methodist Episcopal church caught fire in the 1950s, the historic pipe organ was damaged. However, the organ was carefully repaired and restored, and it continues to be played every Sunday.

The stone church on Grove Street is the Schuylerville Episcopal Church. Some of the other churches in the area include the United Methodist Church of Quaker Springs, the United Methodist Church of Schuylerville, the Old Saratoga Reformed Church, the Assembly of God, St. Stephen's Episcopal Church, the First Baptist Church, and Notre Dame de Lourdes Catholic Church.

Episcopal Church, Schuylerville, N. Y.

The land for the Church of the Visitation was donated by the Victory Manufacturing Company. In 1871, the cornerstone was laid at the corner of Burgoyne and Green Streets in the village of Victory. The church was closed in 1990. The building is now used as a private residence.

This early photograph shows the interior of the Schuylerville water-pumping station, located at the corner of Canal and Ferry Streets. Pictured, from left to right, are as follows: (front row) W.E. Burnett, village clerk; W.T. Scully, village mayor; and A. Trumbull, village trustee; (back row) Elmer Walker, engineer; and ? Reardon and J. Byrnes, contractors.

The Bullard Block is listed in the National Registry of Historic Places. This photograph was taken in the mid-1880s. Today, the building looks much the same as it did then. The Bullard Block is located on Broad Street in Schuylerville.

Dom's Service Station was located on Broad Street, where the Glens Falls National Bank now stands. Dominick Nardelli owned and operated the station. The Ruff family also owned it for a time. The station was demolished and the bank was built in its place.

This photograph shows Walt's Servicecenter before it was purchased by the Ruff family. Walt's was located on South Broad Street. Don Ernst opened the station in 1938. Mintzer's from Mechanicville built the station.

Charlie Dong owned a laundry in Schuylerville. Over the years, he moved the business to several different locations within the village.

Grandma Moses, the famous American painter, attended one of the many activities and celebrations held over the years at the Schuyler House. Pictured on the front porch during this 1952 event are as follows, from left to right: (front row) unidentified, unidentified, Mrs. Harry Carmen, Grandma Moses, unidentified, unidentified, (back row) Betty Barrett, Adeley Bullard, Betty Sherman, Mrs. Bullard, Leora Hills, unidentified, unidentified, Mary Lou Whitney, Mary Pendrak Carr, and Helen Bullard.

93

The Russell Block was located on the southwest corner of Ferry and Broad Streets. The building included residences and businesses, such as B.K. Northrup and the National Express Co. In the mid-1960s, the building burned.

This land on the northwest corner of Broad and Spring Streets has an interesting history. It was the campground for the American soldiers during the Revolutionary War. Here, the Tory spy Lovelass was tried and convicted. The Chubb home occupied the site until 1924, when Larmon House Movers transported it to a Pearl Street location, where it is now the Longo residence. Schuylerville later built a new school on the empty site.

The Naylor home was located on Broad Street in Schuylerville, between the Hotel Schuyler and the former Still Funeral Home. The telephone company bought the property, tore the home down, and built a concrete-block building to house equipment.

In 1912, the Corsetti shoe shop was fully decorated for Historic Week. The shop, which was also the Corsetti residence, was located on South Broad Street.

The Schuylerville Boy Scout troop lined up on Pearl Street in 1913. The scoutmaster was James Orr and the assistant scoutmaster was David Ryan. Troop members included Joe Cromie, Paul Lapierre, Owen Hughes, Pat Grout, Foster Trombley, Harry Drew, Gerald Hughes, Ted Salls, Roland Cromie, Arthur Lapierre, Aimie Lapierre, William Ryan, and Michael Hughes. In the background is Notre Dame de Lourdes Church.

The Thomas Ingham meat market was located on Ferry Street. This early photograph shows prices for some of the goods on the shelves. In later years, Hughie Hughes purchased and operated the market.

The Glass Bakery was known for miles around. Mr. Glass installed snowplows on his trucks so that, even in winter, baked goods would be delivered in a timely manner. The bakery, which was also a restaurant and hotel, was located on Broad Street. This photograph, c. 1930, shows the following employees, from left to right: (front row) Henry Eddy, Kenneth Williams, Henry Pratt, Henry Deguire, Morris Sage, ? Allen, Louise Lahey, Lousinda Granville, Sadie Conley, and Etta Trombley; (back row) Jimmy Salls, Owen Hughes, Edward Bennett, Theodore Salls, Edward Beaulac, Clarence Miles, Charles Wilson, Mickey Hughes, and Ray Moody.

In the work area of the Glass Bakery on Broad Street, employees posed for this photograph, c. 1930. They are, from left to right, Ray Hubbard, Charles Wilson, Kenneth Wilson, Carl Varney, Edward Beaulac, and James Salls. In 1945, the Glass Bakery burned in a fire that was of suspicious origin. According to rumor, a burglar broke in and then set fire to the bakery to destroy any evidence.

Synder's cornfield was located on the south side of Burgoyne Street, just south of the Saratoga Monument.

The reservoir for the Schuylerville water system was constructed at the top of Prospect Hill, almost across from the Saratoga Monument. The contractors for the project were Reardon and Barnet.

This photograph shows workers repairing a canal boat at the dry dock and shipyard in the village of Schuylerville.

Hudson Valley Bridge, crossing Fish Creek, Schuylerville, N. Y.

This photograph shows a Hudson Valley Trolley car crossing the bridge over Fish Creek, at the south end of Broad Street. Also visible are the inlet for water going to the Bullard Paper Mill (right) and the Horicon Mill (left).

Lined up for review are the following Civil War veterans from the 77th Regiment of Saratoga County, from left to right: (front row) the commander Samuel Squires, G.W. Potter, Charles Bartlett Sam Van Order, Willard McCreedy, Lon Hammond, Jim E. Wiliot, Phinious Dixon, George Hammond, Curley Rex Dwyer, Dr. John Strong, Robert Dixon, Ben Northrup, Sam Barrie, J. Jeffords, Morris Sullivan, C. Pease, and George Holmes; (back row, at house) C.H. McNaughton. Many of the veterans were from Schuylerville.

Germain Potter, a Civil War veteran and resident of Schuylerville, posed for this photograph in June 1921.

The General Schuyler hand pumper was owned and used by the Schuyler Hose Company. In 1893, it won an award at the New York State firemen's competition held in Coney Island for shooting water nearly 235 feet.

This Schuylerville school was completed in 1926. The building cost $180,000. It contained 18 classrooms for students in grades 1-12, a gym, an auditorium, a cafeteria, and a kitchen. In later years, two additions were constructed. The building was closed in 1993, after the new Schuylerville Central School was enlarged.

The Union Free School opened in 1876 on the corner of Green and University Streets. The 68-by-72-foot, four-story school cost $15,000 to build. Designed to accommodate up to 350 students, the building was steam heated and contained more than 1,000 volumes in its library, two pianos, and $400 worth of physical and chemical equipment. The school was closed in 1926.

Four

THE VILLAGE OF VICTORY

The residences and businesses of the village of Victory are shown on this 1866 map, printed in the *New Topographical Atlas of Saratoga County, New York*.

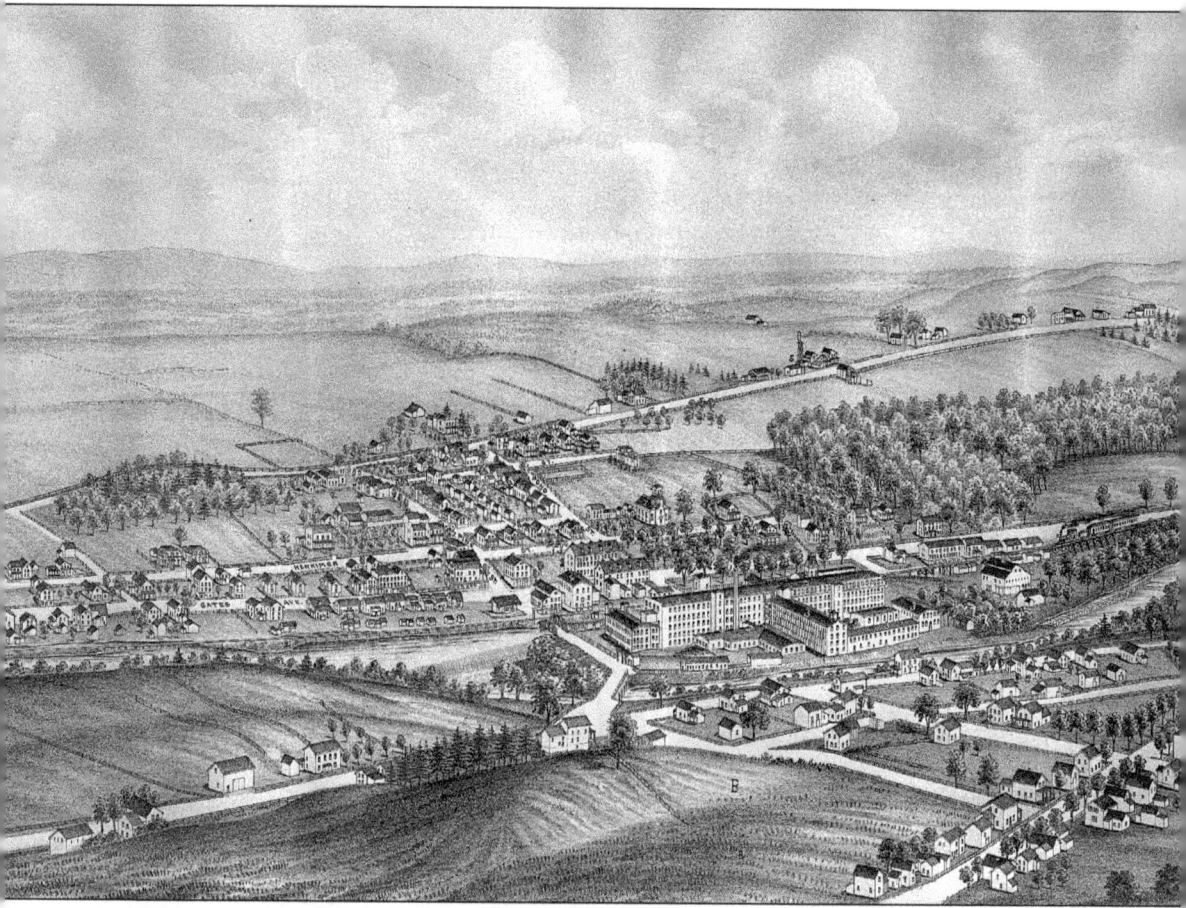

Victory was a thriving community with a prosperous cotton mill and numerous related stores and businesses. This 1889 lithograph shows the location of the mill, businesses, and historical places.

The four-room school in Victory Mills was built in 1872. It was known as Schoolhouse #4 until the schools centralized in the late 1940s. Then it became a part of the Schuylerville Central School. After June 1955, the school was closed. The building currently houses the municipal offices of Victory and the David Nevins Fire Department.

This c. 1940 photograph, shows a close-up view of the Victory Mills school, located on Pine Street.

These fifth- and sixth-grade students at the Victory Mills School in 1947–48 are pictured from left to right as follows: (front row) Nancy Bihn, Donald Casey, Carole Pechette, Kenneth Wood, Sheila Cromie, Wanda Obie; (back row) William White, Harold Sullivan, Edgar White, Gloria Bouchard, and Marion LaPierre. Their teacher was Ella Murray.

This train wreck occurred in the early 1900s, near the village of Victory. The Hoosic Tunnel line eventually became the Fitchburg Railroad and was completed through Victory in 1882.

This photograph shows one of a series of train wrecks that occurred in the Victory area. The Fitchburg Railroad eventually became the Boston and Maine Railroad. The railroad was critical to the Victory Mill operation, since both incoming supplies and finished products were shipped by the train. In addition to freight, the railroad provided passenger service.

Numerous trusses and bridges were built in and around Victory. This photographs shows workers at a railroad trestle just outside the village.

The railroad station in Victory handled both passengers and freight. This view was taken from across Fish Creek, looking northeast.

In 1955, the Victory station was closed and the rail line was discontinued. Beginning the year after that, the railroad tracks were torn up.

The David Nevins Fire Company organized in 1896. It re-organized in the late 1940s as the David Nevins Fire Department. Department members posed with their fire truck in this photograph, c. 1950.

This early hand pumper was used extensively by the David Nevins Fire Department. Now no longer in use, the pumper has been refurbished and is exhibited in parades and at other events.

This Stone Arch Bridge once connected the village of Victory and Smithville. Over the years, the bridge was weakened by erosion and general disrepair. In the 1980s, it was replaced by a beam bridge.

Located on Herkimer Street, the Union Methodist Church was built in 1854 on land donated by the Victory Mill. The Methodist minister from Schuylerville served this church as well as his own. The church was closed in the 1920s.

HONOR ROLL

DAN BARRETT	OMER BOVIN	CHAS. GORDON	HAROLD ELCOX	MARTIN HUCKA
W.M HALL	LOUIS BOVIN JR.	HAVEY GORDON	OCTAVE WOOD	JAS HALEY
JOE REED	DONALD FOWLER	ROY CORMIE	W.M FIELDS	JOHN MITCHELL
WILFRED VENN	LEO HUGHES	JOHN HAREN	WALTER WOOD	CHAS FIELDS JR.
JOHN J. SULLIVAN	MALCOM HARVEY	SILAS HALEY	W.M RIKER	HENRY HUGHES
CHAS. BOVIN	CLEMENT CURRIER	NELSON MOSHER	VICTORIA OBIE	ART STEWART
LENARD NACEY	CYRIL CURRIER	EARL RYAN	ELMER MOSHER	MARSHALL WHITING
EDW. SHRADER	VERNER LaBARGE	JOE HENNESSEY	EDW. MOSHER	LOUIS STEWART
BOB HALEY	FRED LaBARGE JR.	GLEN PRATT	FRANK GORDN	J.E SALLS JR.
ALBERT YOUNG	JOE CROMIE	THOS. NACEY JR.	RBT. SLOANE	M.C SALLS
JOHN MARTIS	GEORGE BIHN	W.M BURCH		THOS. HALEY
GEO. DREW	CHAS. DAVIS	HENRY PURDY		ROBERT PERIARD
NELSON DREW	THOS. COLEMAN	W.M PURDY		C DeGARMO
LARRY VENN	W.M LOOMIS	FRED GRAVELLE		E. DICKSON
HAROLD SHAW	ALBERT LOOMIS	W.M DAVIGNON		W. KNOWLTON
R. OBIE	LEO LANCIER	DONA PERIARD		JOHN SALLS
	EDWARD REED JR.	BERNARD MITCHELL		
	CLEMENT REED	EDW. CANFIELD		
	WILLARD GORDON			
	DONALD McCARTHY			

VILLAGE OF VICTORY MILLS

The Honor Roll for the village of Victory Mills lists the 2 women and 99 men from the village who served in WW II.

DAM AND WATERFALLS AT VICTORY MILLS, N. Y.

The Victory Mill was strategically located to take advantage of the waterpower available on Fish Creek. The mill had its own hydroelectric generating station on site. This photograph shows the dam on Fish Creek and a row of mill houses in the background.

111

The owners of the Victory Mill constructed a number of houses for their workers. This photograph shows some of the row houses located in the village.

The Victory Mills Post Office opened in 1852. The first postmaster was Roland Coffin. The village population was listed as 637 in the census of 1860. This view shows store owner and postmaster Willam Harvey inside the post office in the 1940s.

Victory had some stores and businesses, but not a full range because of its proximity to Schuylerville. This service station was one of several businesses located on Gates Avenue.

The Victory Mill owned this large building on Gates Avenue. It was used for storage and as housing for mill employees.

The Victory Mill was a massive structure, which began operating in 1846. By 1849, the mill produced 1.8 million yards of cotton cloth. The cloth was made on 309 looms with 12,500 spindles. In 1850, the number of employees totaled 160 men and 209 women. Over the years,

the mill was enlarged several times. This photograph of the front of the mill was taken looking south. It dates from the 1880s.

The Victory Mill built and operated a Community House for its employees. There, the company offered free parties, recreation, and health services. The Community House had dances, vaudeville, operas, and a resident nurse. During the flu epidemic of 1914, the Community House served as a hospital.

This photograph shows the rear of the Victory Mill, where some smaller buildings were located.

Bales of cotton for the Victory Mill arrived by rail. This photograph shows workmen unloading the baled cotton from the railroad cars.

Employees at the Victory Mill made millions of yards of cotton cloth, using hundreds of looms and thousands of spindles. This photograph, c. 1900, shows employees working at some of the mill's many looms.

Pictured outside the Victory Mill are some of the employees who worked at the mill in the early 1920s. At the height of its activity, in 1855, the cotton mill employed 104 men,

198 women, 38 boys, and 86 girls.

A concrete addition was built at the Victory Mill site in 1918. The addition greatly increased the production capacity of the mill.

This elevator-like device lifted the concrete used to build the addition at the Victory Mill.

The Victory Mill maintained its own fire department. This photograph, c. 1890, shows some of the earliest members of the department.

In 1928, the owners closed the Victory Mill. The American Manufacturing Company moved south that year and shipped the last of the cotton mill machinery to Alabama in early 1929. The move gave the company access to cheap labor and nearby raw materials. Here in Victory, with its primary employer gone, the village fell on hard times.

Parades have always been popular in the village of Victory. This parade took place in the early 1900s.

Victory celebrated Old Home Week in 1913. In the background is the Union Methodist Church on Herkimer Street.

Located on Gates Avenue, Ingham's Meat Market and post office was once a regular stop for village residents.

This 1952 photograph shows the former Victory Mill when it was owned by United Board and Carton Corporation. The company made folding cartons, many of which were shipped by rail. In 1972, Wheelabrator-Frye Incorporated purchased the carton plant for its graphics communication group, the A.L. Garber Company.

Over the years, the older parts of the mill were torn down. Some of the bricks from the mill were loaded on pallets and shipped to Boston, where they were used in the renovation of some of the city's old buildings.

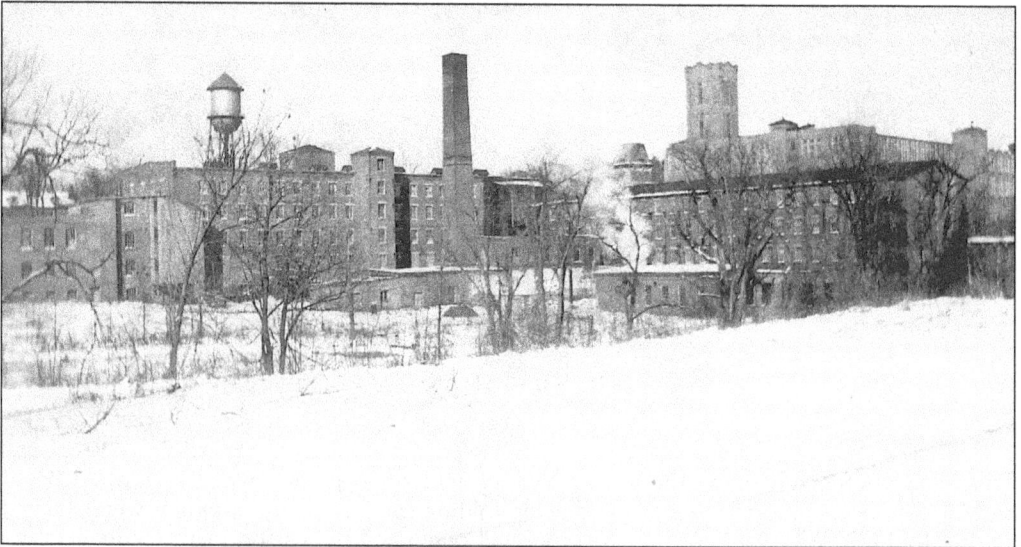

This photograph of the Victory Mill, including the water tower, was taken from Smithville.

After it went out of use, the water tower of the Victory Mill became a hazard and had to be torn down.

This is a front view of the village's new post office. In the late 1800s, the town had six post offices. One was located in Victory and the others were in Schuylerville, Quaker Springs, Grangerville, Coveville, and Deans Corners.

As the David Nevins Fire Department acquired more and larger-sized equipment, it outgrew the original firehouse shown in this photograph.

A local resident painted a sign announcing the Fireman's Bazaar in Victory Mills.

This building on Gates Avenue in Victory contained several residences.

Before the days of refrigeration, ice was cut from ponds in the winter, stored in icehouses, and then delivered to customers as needed. This photograph shows blocks of ice neatly loaded on a horse-drawn sled. The Victory Mill is visible in the background.

The end of the school year was always a special event. In this early photograph, young students holding college pennants participated in a graduation ceremony at the Victory grade school.

www.ingramcontent.com/pod-product-compliance
Lightning Source LLC
Chambersburg PA
CBHW080848100426
42812CB00007B/1958